science
essentials

The perfect **exam revision** guide

reproduction, breathing & health

Denise Walker

First published in paperback in 2010 by:
Evans Brothers
2a Portman Mansions
Chiltern Street
London W1U 6NR

Series editor:
Harriet Brown

Editor:
Harriet Brown

Design:
Simon Morse
Adam Williams

Illustrations:
Q2A Creative

Printed in China

British Library Cataloguing in
Publication Data

Walker, Denise
  Reproduction, breathing and
health. - (Science essentials.
  Biology)
  1.Reproduction - Juvenile literature
2.Respiration -
  Juvenile literature 3.Health -
Juvenile literature
  I.Title
  571.8

ISBN: 9780237539771

Contents

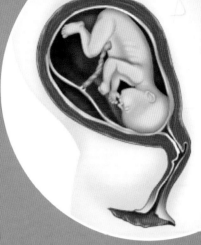

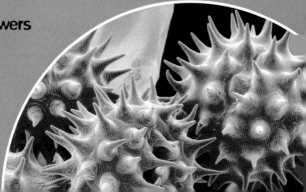

Introduction

We all begin life as a sperm cell from our father and an egg cell from our mother. From this point on, we grow and develop through birth, childhood, adolescence, and into adulthood.

This book takes you on a journey to discover more about how this incredible process happens. Learn about how the male and female reproductive systems work. Find out all about the menstrual cycle, contraception, pregnancy and birth.

Discover how after birth we are able to breathe for ourselves and gain energy from our food. Learn about the ways in which our bodies try to prevent and fight infection to stay healthy. You can also find out about how famous scientists, like Edward Jenner, used their scientific and observational skills to prevent disease.

This book also contains feature boxes that will help you to unravel more about the mysteries of reproduction, breathing and health. Test yourself on what you have learnt so far; investigate some of the concepts discussed; find out more key facts; and discover some of the scientific findings of the past and how these might be utilised in the future.

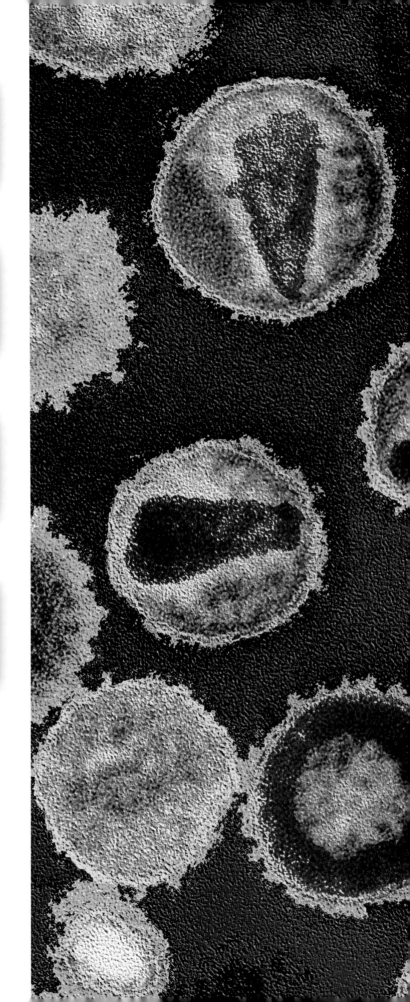

Did you know?

▶ Watch out for these boxes – they contain surprising and fascinating facts about reproduction, breathing and health.

Test yourself

▶ Use these boxes to see how much you've learnt. Try to answer the questions without looking at the book, but take a look if you are really stuck.

Investigate

▶ These boxes contain experiments that you can carry out at home. The equipment you will need is usually cheap and easy to find around the home.

Time travel

▶ These boxes describe scientific discoveries from the past and fascinating developments that pave the way for the advance of science in the future.

Answers

At the end of this book on pages 46 and 47, you will find the answers to the questions from the 'Test yourself' and 'Investigate' boxes.

Glossary

Words highlighted in **bold** are described in detail in the glossary on pages 46 and 47.

Growing up

From before we are born, until adulthood is reached, we grow and change. While we are young, medical experts check that our growth is normal. Once adulthood is reached, we do not grow any taller, but our bodies and minds continue to change. But why do we grow, what controls our growth and how can we expect to change in the future?

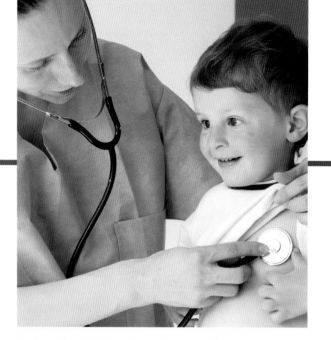

▲ Pre-school children have their growth and development checked on a regular basis.

BLUEPRINT FOR GROWTH

Although everyone has his or her own growth rate, most people follow the same general growth pattern. A **hormone** called **human growth hormone** is responsible for the growth of bones, muscles and tissues. Hormones are chemical messengers that are produced by glands and carried in the blood. Human growth hormone is released by the pituitary gland in the brain.

Pituitary gland

If the pituitary gland releases too little of the hormone, growth is stunted, and if it releases too much, growth is rapid and extreme. In most people, there is the right amount of human growth hormone, which means that the individual follows a normal growth pattern. Human growth hormone is released faster during sleep so it is especially important that the young have plenty of rest.

Normal growth does not only rely on human growth hormone. Environmental factors, such as good nutrition and health, also affect growth patterns.

◄ The pituitary gland sits at the bottom of the brain and is the size of a pea. Amongst other hormones, it produces human growth hormone and 'feel-good' hormones called endorphins.

GROWTH PATTERNS

Human growth can be divided into five stages:

(1) Before birth	During this time there is massive change as a simple ball of cells grows and develops into a baby that is ready to be born (see pages 22-23).
(2) Infancy	This is the time from birth until a child has been fully weaned (begins to eat foods other than milk). This is usually up to one year of age. There is a **growth spurt** during this time. A growth spurt is a period of very rapid growth. At birth, babies are about 50 centimetres long, and during the first year the growth rate is approximately 20 centimetres per year.
(3) Childhood	This is the time following infancy during which boys and girls show few differences. On average, the growth rate is 10 centimetres per year between the ages of one and two, and after this it drops to around five centimetres per year.
(4) Puberty and **adolescence**	This usually happens in the teenage years, during which boys and girls begin to develop sexual characteristics (see pages 9-13). Another growth spurt occurs during this period and the growth rate rises to 10 centimetres per year.
(5) Adulthood	This is the longest period of change. Although after the age of 21 the pituitary gland does not release much human growth hormone, adults change in other ways. As the body ages, hair colour and distribution, skin texture, and agility may change. After the age of 50, people lose muscle mass. Elderly people may become shorter. Surprisingly, noses and ears are thought to continue to grow throughout adulthood.

During growth from infancy to adulthood, head size does not change much at all. The rest of the body does most of the growing. This is why young babies may look out of proportion. In fact, the head of a newborn baby makes up roughly one quarter of a baby's height, whereas in an adult it makes up about one eighth.

GROWTH OF THE HEAD AND BODY

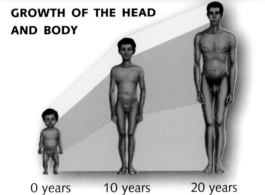

0 years   10 years   20 years

◀ Head size increases very little in comparison with the growth the rest of the body undergoes.

HUMAN GROWTH RATES

▶ This graph shows how height changes with time.

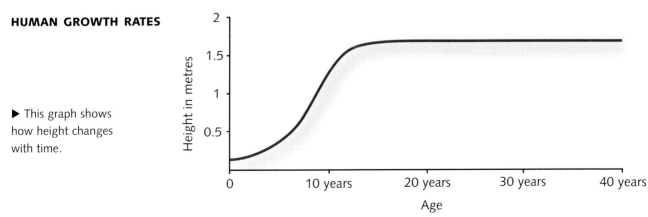

7

THE EARLY YEARS (0-5 YEARS)

During this period of growth, there are massive mental and physical changes:

Age	Changes
Birth	Babies are born relatively undeveloped so that the head is not too big to be born.
6 weeks	Babies sleep for most of the time, but they can follow objects with their eyes and listen to the sound of people talking.
6 months	Babies can hold their heads up and keep their backs straight. They can also hold objects and squeal or babble. Surprising research has also shown that babies may have an extremely basic understanding of numbers.
8 months	Babies can sit completely unsupported and turn towards familiar voices. They can also copy simple sounds.
10 months	Babies begin to crawl and may pull themselves into a standing position. Their first words are spoken around this time.
14 months	At this age, children can stand unsupported and may be able to walk without help. They may speak a few words and can certainly indicate what they want or need.
2 years	Two- to three-years-olds can run and jump, turn the pages of a book, identify familiar objects and form a few short sentences.
4 years	Four-year-olds usually have relatively good balance and can hop from one foot to the other. They can draw simple pictures and can dress and undress themselves.

GOING TO SCHOOL (5-10 YEARS)

In many parts of the world, children start school around the age of five. The child's mind develops a lot during this period. Imaginative role-play games help the child to learn about the world. Children are quick to learn and copy the behaviour of their adult role models.

DID YOU KNOW?

▶ The wrist of an adult contains more bones than that of a newborn baby. Many 'bones' in a newborn baby are made almost entirely of cartilage. Cartilage does not show up on an x-ray. By the age of five or six, the cartilage has changed into bone. Bones show up on an x-ray because they are denser than cartilage. The photograph shows a three-year-old's wrist (above right) and an adult's wrist (below right).

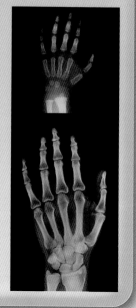

▶ Parents who believe that their babies have grown overnight may be correct. Scientists have discovered that babies often do not grow at all for several days or weeks. Then, they suddenly grow between five and 16.5 millimetres in less than one day.

TURNING INTO AN ADULT (10-15 YEARS)

The stage of life when the human sex organs begin to work is called **puberty**. Large amounts of sex hormones cause the onset of puberty. These hormones can also affect a person's mood and emotions, which can make this a confusing and difficult time. This stage of growth and development is called adolescence. Scientists have also discovered that at puberty, some regions of the brain re-organise themselves.

Changes in boys

The **primary sexual characteristics** – the sex organs – are present from birth in both males and females. In males between the ages of 12 and 16, the testes begin to secrete a sex hormone called testosterone. Testosterone causes the male **secondary sexual characteristics** to develop:

(1) The testes develop and produce sperm cells. Sperm cells are also called sex cells or **gametes**.

(2) Hair grows on the face, under the arms, in the pubic region and sometimes on the chest.

(3) The voice deepens.

(4) Muscles develop, which often gives males a larger size than females.

Changes in girls

At puberty, between the ages of 11 and 15, a girl's ovaries begin to secrete a sex hormone called oestrogen. Oestrogen causes the female secondary sexual characteristics to develop:

(1) The ovaries begin to release an ovum (egg cell) each month. Ova are also called sex cells or gametes. This means the menstrual cycle begins (see page 14-15) and a female is physically ready to have children.

(2) Hair grows under the arms and in the pubic region.

(3) Breasts begin to enlarge.

(4) Hips widen.

Test yourself

▶ What is a growth spurt and when do they happen?

▶ List the secondary sexual characteristics of adolescent males and females.

BOY

MAN

GIRL

WOMAN

Becoming an adult (15-20 years)

By the age of 15, most of the physical changes that make us adults are complete. However, emotional development is usually not complete. During the late teenage years, adolescents begin to think more for themselves and to take responsibility for their actions. They become increasingly independent from their parents or carers, and many have their first sexual relationship.

The male reproductive system

Growth and development from birth to adulthood takes between 20 and 23 years in humans. In both males and females, the biological changes prepare us to become parents. In males, the purpose of the reproductive system is to make sperm cells, store them until they are required, and then to deliver them to the site of **fertilisation** in the female.

TESTES (SINGULAR – TESTICLE OR TESTIS)

Inside the testes there are numerous coiled tubes, which produce sperm cells. Sperm production is most efficient at 34-35°C. Human core body temperature is around 37°C. To keep the sperm cool, the testes hang outside of the body in a sac of skin. The testes are positioned between the legs so that they experience as little physical damage as possible.

Testosterone is produced in the cells between the coiled tubes. From puberty until death, sperm are constantly manufactured, but they are only released during **ejaculation**.

THE MALE REPRODUCTIVE SYSTEM

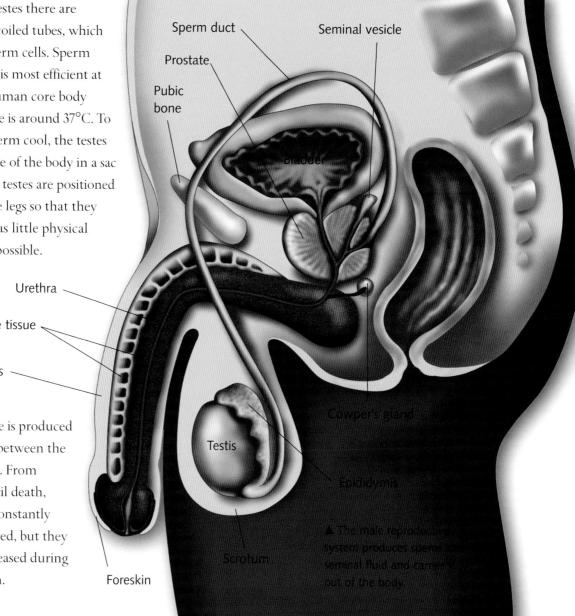

Sperm duct

Seminal vesicle

Prostate

Pubic bone

Bladder

Urethra

Erectile tissue

Penis

Cowper's gland

Testis

Epididymis

Scrotum

Foreskin

▲ The male reproductive system produces sperm and seminal fluid and carries it out of the body.

SCROTUM (SCROTAL SAC)

The testes are enclosed within a sac of skin called the scrotum.

EPIDIDYMIS

The epididymis is situated just outside the testes and is also a series of coiled tubes. Mature sperm from the testes are stored here.

SPERM DUCT (VAS DEFERENS)

Mature sperm cells leave the testes by the sperm duct. The sperm duct connects the testes to another tube called the urethra.

SEMINAL VESICLE, COWPER'S GLAND AND PROSTATE GLAND

These three structures work together to produce a fluid called seminal fluid. As sperm travels from the testes past these structures, seminal fluid is added. The mixture is now called **semen**. Semen is approximately 99.5 per cent seminal fluid and 0.5 per cent sperm cells. Seminal fluid is made up from the following substances:

(1) Mucus – this lubricates the penis during sexual intercourse.
(2) A sugar called fructose – this provides a source of energy for the sperm cells. Once they leave the male body they need energy to swim towards the ovum.
(3) Alkaline substance – this helps the sperm cells to survive once they enter the female body.

URETHRA

The urethra has two roles:
(1) It carries semen from the sperm duct, through the penis, to the outside world.
(2) It carries urine from the bladder, through the penis, for excretion.

A valve in the urethra prevents these functions from happening at the same time. Because the male excretory system and reproductive system are positioned so close together, they are often referred to as the urinogenital system.

PENIS

The penis is made from soft, spongy tissue. During sexual arousal, the air spaces can fill up with blood, which makes the penis hard and erect. This is necessary before it can be inserted into the female. The tip of the penis is called the glans and is very sensitive. The glans is responsible for triggering the journey of the sperm cells from the epididymis. A layer of skin called the foreskin protects the glans. In some cultures, the foreskin is removed from baby males in a procedure called circumcision.

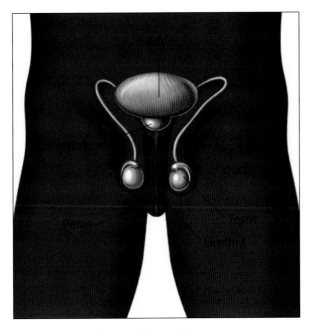

▲ A front view of the male reproductive system.

TEST YOURSELF

▶ Write down, in the correct order, the structures through which a sperm cell passes on its journey from the testes to the female body.

The female reproductive system

Unlike boys, girls are born with all of the sex cells they will release during a lifetime, but these are present in an immature form. The female reproductive system is designed to: (1) produce and release mature ova, (2) receive male sperm, (3) provide a place for the sperm and ova to come together, and (4) to provide a place for a developing baby to grow before birth.

OVARIES

The ovaries are a key part of the female reproductive system. They not only produce ova, but also secrete some of the sex hormones that control female reproduction. At birth, the two ovaries contain up to 450,000 ova. At puberty, the ova begin to mature. Oestrogen triggers the mature ova to be released from the ovary. Usually only one ovum is released each month.

FUNNELS OF THE OVIDUCTS

Ova are released from the ovaries and captured by these funnels.

OVIDUCTS (FALLOPIAN TUBES)

These tubes connect the funnels to the uterus. They are lined with small hairs that wave around and push the ovum along. It can take up to seven days for an ovum to reach the uterus. However, if sperm are

THE FEMALE REPRODUCTIVE SYSTEM

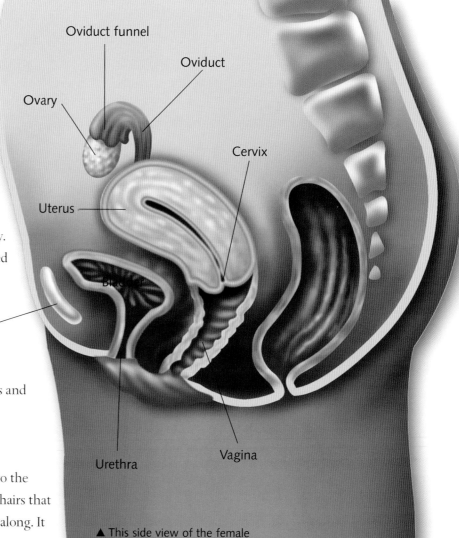

▲ This side view of the female reproductive system shows just one of the two ovaries and oviducts.

DAYS 14-21 RECEPTIVE PHASE

By this point in the cycle, the uterus lining is thick enough to receive a fertilised ovum. The best conditions for implantation of an embryo into the uterus occur between six and seven days after ovulation. This is approximately the length of the receptive phase.

DAYS 21-28 PRE-MENSTRUAL PHASE

The sex hormone progesterone is released to make the uterus lining stronger in case an ovum has been fertilised. This is the time during which a woman may experience pre-menstrual syndrome (PMS). Progesterone can affect a woman's behaviour and make her moody, weepy or unpredictable. If fertilisation has not occurred by the end of this period, the uterus lining breaks down and menstruation begins. If fertilisation has occurred, the uterus lining remains thick and a pregnancy begins.

UNPROTECTED SEX

An ovum can take up to seven days to travel from the ovary to the uterus. During this time, if sperm is present the female could become pregnant. Sperm cells can survive outside of the male body for on average three days, but they can survive for up to seven days. This extends the period during which a female can become pregnant. This period is called the 'unsafe' period because if unprotected sex occurs, pregnancy is highly likely. The female body can also be very unpredictable. An ovum can be released at any time of the month. Therefore, to avoid a pregnancy there is no time during which unprotected sex could be considered 'safe'.

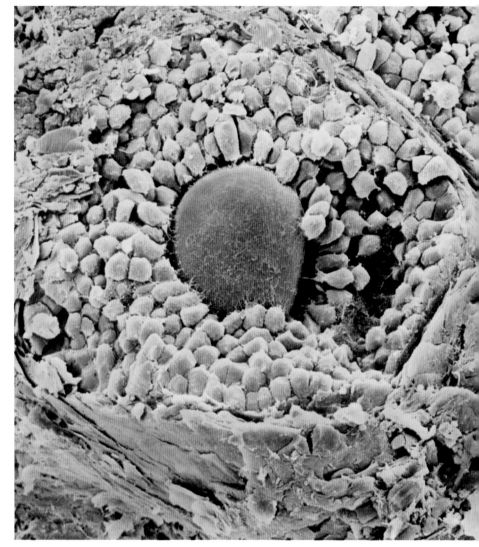

▲ This ovum (the central red sphere) is developing inside a follicle, inside an ovary. Once it is fully mature it will be released around day 15 of the menstrual cycle. The magnification of this image is x400.

DID YOU KNOW?

▶ Women who live together often have their period (menstruation) at almost exactly the same time. Scientists believe that women release pheromones. A pheromone is a chemical that influences the behaviour or functioning of another individual. Several studies have demonstrated that pheromones cause the alignment of women's menstrual cycles if they spend a lot of time together.

Fertilisation

In most organisms, when male and female sex cells meet, fertilisation occurs. In humans, fertilisation is the fusion of a man's sperm and a woman's ovum. Sperm is ejected into the vagina during sexual intercourse. Millions of sperm are released at once, but only one is required for fertilisation.

CHOOSING A PARTNER

People can be attracted to each other both physically and emotionally. You may be attracted to a celebrity, or a boy or girl in your class. Scientists have researched why people are attracted by some, but not others. Some suggest that pheromones have an influence on our attraction to others. It is widely known that

pheromones play an important role in the animal world. For example, male mice secrete a pheromone that encourages sexual development in nearby females.

However, pheromones do not explain why you might be attracted to someone you've never met, such as a film or television star. Some scientists believe that without realising it, we are attracted to people with characteristics that we'd like to pass on to our offspring. Features such as a strong frame in men, and a shapely figure in women, could indicate that an individual is ideally suited for reproduction. However, there are no hard and fast rules. Features that attract some people may be equally off-putting to others. Relationships

depend on an enormous number of factors such as physical and emotional preferences, shared interests and common goals.

SEXUAL INTERCOURSE

For many people, sexual intercourse is a normal part of a stable relationship. Choosing when to begin a sexual relationship varies between individuals. Before sexual intercourse can take place, the man becomes excited, and his penis fills with blood to produce an erection. Once the penis is hard, it is easier to insert it into the woman's vagina. This is called **copulation**.

During sexual intercourse, the male stimulates his penis by sliding it in and out of the vagina. When stimulation is great enough, sperm cells and seminal fluid are ejected into the vagina. This process is called ejaculation and the man will experience a pleasurable feeling called an orgasm.

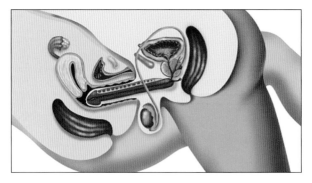

▲ During sexual intercourse, the man ejaculates semen into the vagina.

The woman may also feel an orgasm as a result of the repeated rubbing of the penis against her clitoris.

MEETING OF SEX CELLS

Ejaculation occurs with great force so that the sperm cells are deposited at the top of the vagina in the cervix. Egg cells are large in comparison to sperm cells and so are easier to find. Under a microscope, sperm cells look like little tadpoles. Millions of sperm swim up the uterus and into the oviducts to find the ovum.

When a sperm cell reaches the ovum, its head enters while the tail breaks off and gets left behind. The nucleus (the part that contains the genetic information) of the sperm then joins with the nucleus of the ovum. A zygote is formed and fertilisation has now occurred. The surface of the ovum changes so that no more sperm cells can enter.

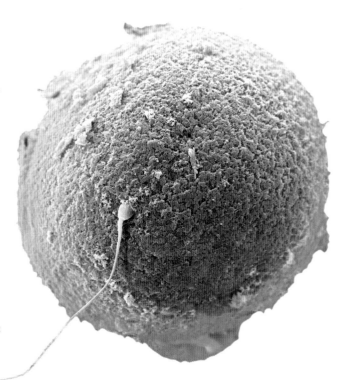

▲ Only one tiny sperm can penetrate the ovum. The magnification of this image is approximately x700.

Zygote

JOURNEY ALONG THE OVIDUCT

The zygote travels along the oviduct and begins to divide. Very quickly, the zygote becomes a ball of many cells. After approximately six days, the zygote reaches the uterus and implants in the thickly lined wall. This embedding is called **conception** and pregnancy now begins.

EGG CELL DIVISION

TEST YOURSELF

▶ During sexual intercourse, in what order do the following processes happen?

Ejaculation and orgasm
Fertilisation
Erection
Copulation
Conception

▲ An ovum begins as one cell. It divides in two. Each of the two resulting cells divide, and so on. Very rapidly a ball of many cells forms.

IVF

Some couples have difficulties conceiving children. There are several techniques that can help couples in this situation. One of these techniques is *in-vitro* fertilisation (IVF). *In-vitro* fertilisation means 'fertilisation in glass'. Babies created in this way are sometimes referred to as test-tube babies. The world's first IVF baby was born in the UK in 1978 and today, more than a million have been born worldwide.

WHAT STOPS PREGNANCIES OCCURRING NATURALLY?

There are a variety of reasons why a couple may not be able to conceive a child naturally. In women, reasons include ovulation problems, twisted oviducts or damage to the oviduct as a result of a sexually transmitted disease (STD).

In men, a low sperm count or poor sperm quality reduces fertility. A sperm count is the number of useful sperm found in every centimetre cubed of semen. Within this volume there may also be a number of sperm cells that are not useful. They may have bent or broken tails, or two heads. These deformities mean that the sperm cannot swim well or successfully fertilise the ovum. A normal sperm count is more than 20 million useful sperm in one centimetre cubed of semen.

The age or lifestyle of a couple can also affect fertility. Smoking and drinking alcohol affect fertility in both men and women. Male smokers or drinkers risk damage to the quality of their sperm. Women smokers have only 72 per cent of the fertility of non-smokers. Beyond the age of 35, a woman becomes less fertile. Stress also affects the fertility of both men and women.

TREATING INFERTILITY WITHOUT IVF

In the most straightforward of cases, couples can improve their fertility by changing their lifestyles. Some infertility problems can be treated with medication. For example, a drug can be given to women, which stimulates the ovaries to produce ova. This is called super-ovulation. However, in some cases this is not successful and IVF may then be attempted.

▼ This abnormal sperm is immature and will not develop properly. It is not able to fertilise an ovum.

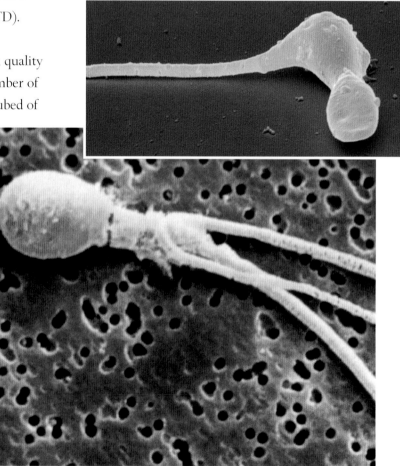

▲ This sperm has three tails. It is unable to swim to the ovum because its tails are too heavy.

How does IVF work?

Carefully measured doses of fertility drugs are given to encourage ova to mature. The development of the ova is monitored using ultrasound.

The woman may be given a general anaesthetic and ova are collected through the vagina or abdomen (belly) using a camera and needle. Active sperm are taken from the male partner's semen and mixed with the ova. The ova become fertilised and divide for several days.

Healthy embryos are replaced in the woman's body through the vagina. The woman is treated with hormones prior to this to make sure she is physically ready to receive the embryos.

Disadvantages of IVF

Recent statistics show that just 27 per cent of IVF treatment cycles result in a birth. This can be a very difficult and upsetting time for the couple. In many countries, IVF is extremely expensive and this limits the number of times treatment cycles can be undergone.

In addition, the risk of an ectopic pregnancy is higher with IVF. Ectopic pregnancies occur when the embryo implants into the oviduct instead of the uterus. All ectopic pregnancies are dangerous and must be terminated because they may cause the oviduct to rupture.

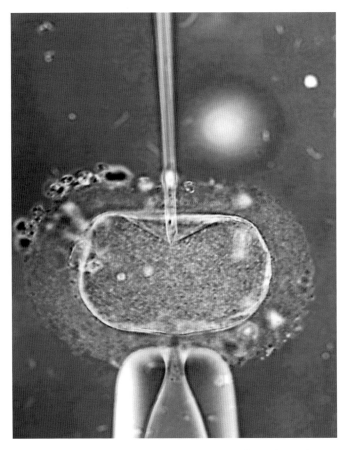

▲ Sometimes, if the egg and sperm will not fuse when they are mixed, the sperm is instead injected directly into the egg.

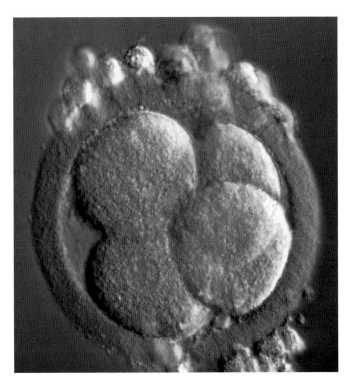

▶ At this stage, when the fertilised egg contains four cells, it is checked to see whether it is of a high enough quality to be put back into the woman. This is a good specimen.

Contraception

Couples do not want to risk the woman becoming pregnant every time they have sexual intercourse. To prevent pregnancy, they use a method of contraception. Contraception means 'against conceiving'. Couples often discuss the different methods of contraception and decide which is best for them. Whichever method is chosen, contraception is the responsibility of both partners and should be discussed openly as part of a mature relationship.

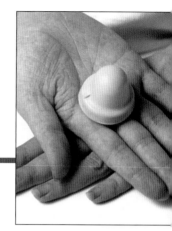

DIFFERENT TYPES OF CONTRACEPTION

Contraception can be:

Physical, such as condoms, a diaphragm, an IUD or a femidom

Chemical, such as the female contraceptive pill and spermicide

Surgical, such as the male vasectomy and female sterilisation

Natural, such as the withdrawal and rhythm methods

CONDOMS

A condom is a thin rubber covering that is placed over the erect penis. When the male wears a condom during intercourse, the ejaculate is caught in the end of the condom. This prevents sperm from entering the vagina. The condom also stops the penis from coming into direct contact with the vagina, which can prevent the spread of STDs.

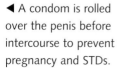

◄ A condom is rolled over the penis before intercourse to prevent pregnancy and STDs.

DIAPHRAGM (CAP)

This is a thin rubber barrier that the woman places over the cervix before intercourse. The diaphragm must be used with a spermicide, which is a cream that kills sperm cells. The diaphragm is an effective contraceptive but must be made to measure at a family planning clinic.

▲ The cap does not protect against STDs.

IUD (INTRAUTERINE DEVICE)

This is a small plastic-coated coil, which is fitted in the uterus where it remains for months or years. It must be fitted by a medical expert. The coil prevents fertilised ova from implanting into the uterus.

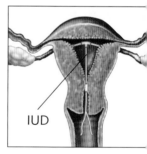

IUD

▲ An IUD prevents zygotes from implanting by irritating the uterus wall.

FEMIDOM

The femidom is a thin sheath that sits inside the vagina during sexual intercourse. It has a closed end to prevent ejaculated sperm from reaching the uterus.

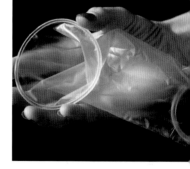

▲ A femidom

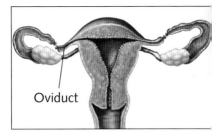

CONTRACEPTIVE PILL

There are three types of contraceptive pill.

The mini-pill contains progestogen (a synthetic version of progesterone) and prevents a fertilised ovum from implanting in the uterus. The combined pill contains synthetic oestrogen and progestogen, and prevents the ovaries from releasing ova. Both of these pills must be taken every day to remain effective. The mini-pill must be taken at precisely the same time every day. The third type of pill is called the morning-after pill. This pill can be used up to 72 hours after unprotected intercourse. This pill prevents any fertilised ova from implanting into the uterus.

VASECTOMY

In later life, some men decide they no longer wish to father children. They may undergo an operation called a vasectomy. A surgeon cuts the sperm ducts and ties them. This means that sperm produced in the testes cannot be released through the penis. Normal sexual intercourse can continue and the body reabsorbs any sperm produced in the testes. This method of contraception is usually permanent although some reversal operations are successful.

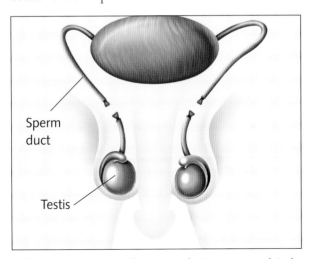

▲ During a vasectomy the sperm ducts are cut and tied, or cut and then stitched closed.

FEMALE STERILISATION

During this operation, the oviducts are cut and tied. This prevents the ova from meeting sperm. Sterilisation is a permanent method of contraception.

▲ Sterilisation is not carried out on young women in case they change their mind and want to have a child in the future.

WITHDRAWAL

This involves the male withdrawing his penis before ejaculation has occurred during sexual intercourse. This method is very unreliable because before ejaculation, small amounts of sperm can leak into the vagina and lead to a pregnancy.

RHYTHM METHOD

Couples who use this method avoid having intercourse during the most fertile parts of the menstrual cycle – just before, during and after an ovum is released. At ovulation, a woman's temperature rises slightly. Couples can monitor the temperature, estimate when an ovum is released and avoid unprotected sex at this time. This method can be very unreliable.

HOW SUCCESSFUL ARE THESE METHODS?

Method of contraception	Effectiveness (per cent)
Physical	92-98
Chemical	99
Natural	80
Surgical	Almost 100

Some people do not use contraception because it is against their religion. Avoiding contraception makes it likely that the woman will become pregnant, and can put both partners at risk of catching an STD.

Pregnancy and birth

Most people spend a long period of their lives using contraceptives and avoiding pregnancy. However, eventually they may make the decision to become a parent. It can take many months of unprotected sexual intercourse for a woman to become pregnant – or it can happen the very first time. Pregnancy is divided into three equal stages called **trimesters**. Human pregnancy lasts around 40 weeks and is controlled by hormones.

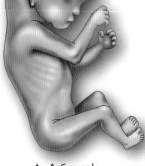

▲ A 6-week old embryo

FIRST TRIMESTER (1-12 WEEKS)

At conception, the 'baby' is a ball of cells smaller than a pinhead. During the first eight weeks, the baby is called an embryo. The embryo floats in a sac filled with amniotic fluid. The fluid cushions and protects the embryo. By week eight, the embryo's heart is functioning, and the brain, limbs and spinal cord are beginning to form. It is now called a foetus. By the end of the first trimester, the foetus's organs, limbs and tissues have formed and it is around seven centimetres long.

SECOND TRIMESTER (13-28 WEEKS)

The foetus has recognisable features such as hands and is able to flex its fingers and suck its thumb. The organs and tissues mature and the foetus grows to around 28 centimetres long.

THIRD TRIMESTER (29-40 WEEKS)

The foetus undergoes its final growth spurt and by birth, will be around 50 centimetres long. A few weeks before the birth, the foetus becomes 'engaged'. This means that it turns so that its head points downward and fits snugly in the mother's pelvis.

▲ A 20-week old foetus

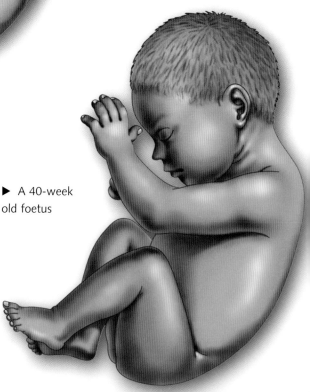

▶ A 40-week old foetus

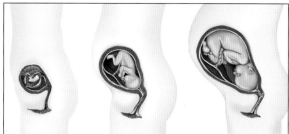

1st trimester   2nd trimester   3rd trimester

▲ Even though a woman's belly expands to accommodate the growing foetus, by 40 weeks, conditions for the baby are cramped and it must tightly fold its arms and legs.

NOURISHING THE FOETUS

The foetus gains all its food and oxygen from the mother during pregnancy. These substances travel from the mother's blood to the foetus through a structure called the placenta. The placenta is attached to the foetus by the umbilical cord. Around 600 millilitres of maternal blood passes through the placenta every minute. As well as carrying nutrition and oxygen to the foetus, the cord also carries away waste produced by the foetus.

The maternal and foetal blood does not mix. Mixing of the blood can be fatal. In addition, the higher blood pressure in the mother could damage the fragile foetal blood vessels.

▼ Oxygen passes from mother to foetus. Waste passes from the foetus to the mother.

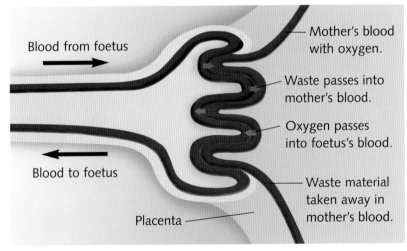

Blood from foetus

Blood to foetus

Placenta

Mother's blood with oxygen.

Waste passes into mother's blood.

Oxygen passes into foetus's blood.

Waste material taken away in mother's blood.

The vessels of the two blood supplies run very closely together and substances **diffuse** across the border from one side to the other.

CHILDBIRTH

Childbirth, or labour, has three stages:

(1) The first stage of labour usually takes between two and 18 hours. The powerful muscles of the uterus begin to contract. The bag of fluid around the baby bursts – the woman's waters have broken. The contractions widen the cervix in preparation for the birth of the baby. When the cervix is 10 centimetres wide, the baby is ready to be born.

(2) The baby is usually delivered headfirst during this stage of labour. The contractions are very strong and force the baby from the uterus through the vagina. Once the head passes through the vagina, the rest of the body follows more easily.

(3) The placenta detaches itself from the uterus and is delivered through the vagina up to an hour after delivery. The umbilical cord is cut and tied.

Substances that can pass from mother to foetus	Substances that can pass from foetus to mother
Oxygen	
Nutrients	Waste products such as carbon dioxide and urea
Antibodies (see page 39)	
Alcohol and some drugs	
Viruses such as rubella	

DID YOU KNOW?

▶ Hormones released during pregnancy can affect a woman's moods and emotions. However, scientists have found that men may also experience a hormonal roller coaster. One study measured hormones in pregnant women and their partners. Surprisingly, the male partners also had increased hormone levels. The researchers suggested that the woman's hormones and pheromones had influenced the male to produce his own hormones.

Breathing

Immediately after birth, a newborn child can breathe for itself. It has a fully formed respiratory system. It can supply its own oxygen needs and rid itself of the waste product, carbon dioxide. The lungs are the main respiratory organs. Their structure allows humans to gain enough oxygen to carry out all of the body processes, such as movement, growth and thought.

THE RESPIRATORY SYSTEM

The human respiratory system is located in the rib cage and is protected by the ribs and breastbone. It has two functions:

(1) It takes oxygen from the air and delivers it to the body.

(2) It removes carbon dioxide from the body and returns it to the air.

This replacement of gases is called **gaseous exchange**.

When we breathe in, air travels through the trachea (windpipe). The trachea splits in two. One half branches to the right and the other half branches left. The branches are called the bronchi. The bronchi lead onto smaller tubes called bronchioles, which are very finely branched. At the end of the bronchioles are structures called alveoli. Alveoli look like tiny bunches of grapes and it is within these structures that gaseous exchange occurs. Each alveolus is just 0.2 millimetres in diameter and each lung contains around 300 million alveoli.

The rib cage covers the lungs. Intercostal muscles are attached to the ribs. When they contract they cause the rib cage to move.

At the bottom of the lungs is another muscle called the diaphragm. At rest, the diaphragm is a dome shaped muscle. It separates the lungs from other important organs, but also helps draw air into the lungs.

▼ Air travels in through the nose and mouth, down the trachea, through the two bronchi, into the bronchioles and finally into the alveoli.

THE RESPIRATORY SYSTEM

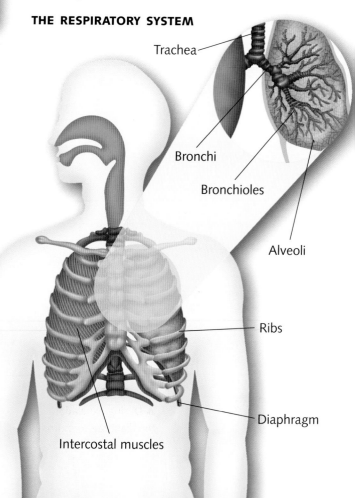

Trachea

Bronchi

Bronchioles

Alveoli

Ribs

Diaphragm

Intercostal muscles

GETTING AIR INTO THE LUNGS

At rest, you inhale (breathe in) about eight litres of air each minute. When you exercise, this can rise to between 88 and 114 litres. This happens because during exercise the muscles need more oxygen to work properly.

Place the palms of your hands over your rib cage and take in a deep breath of air. What happens? Your rib cage moves your hands upwards and outwards. What you cannot feel is that the diaphragm also moves. The diaphragm contracts and flattens, which pulls downwards on the lung space. This movement increases the volume of the lungs. This decreases the pressure in the lungs and air rushes in to equal the pressure inside and outside the lungs.

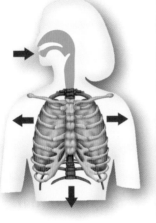

▲ During inhalation, the diaphragm contracts and flattens.

GETTING AIR OUT OF THE LUNGS

Place your hands over your ribs again; inhale and then exhale. As you exhale you should feel your ribs fall back to their original position. The diaphragm reverts to its dome shape. The lung space decreases in volume, which increases the pressure in the lungs. This forces the air out of the lungs.

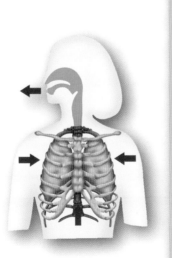

▲ During exhalation, the diaphragm returns to its domed shape.

INVESTIGATE

▶ You may have carried out the bell jar experiment at school. Look at the diagram of the apparatus below. When the rubber sheet is pulled down, the balloons inflate. When the rubber sheet is pushed up, the balloons flatten. Explain how this works in terms of volume and air pressure. In your explanation, include what each part of the experiment represents. There is one way in which this model does not represent the respiratory system. What is this?

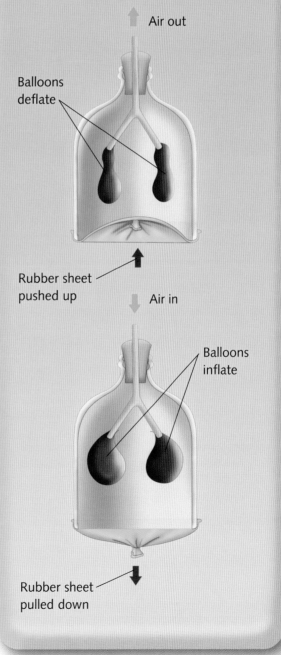

Air out

Balloons deflate

Rubber sheet pushed up

Air in

Balloons inflate

Rubber sheet pulled down

INHALED AIR AND EXHALED AIR

This table shows the content of inhaled and exhaled air.

Component	Inhaled air (per cent)	Exhaled air (per cent)
Oxygen	21	18
Carbon dioxide	0.04	3
Nitrogen	78	78
Water vapour	Variable	Saturated
Temperature	Variable	37°C

OXYGEN – Exhaled air contains only three per cent less oxygen than inhaled air. This small amount of oxygen is enough to meet the body's oxygen demands at rest.

CARBON DIOXIDE – More carbon dioxide is exhaled than inhaled. This is because our lungs remove waste carbon dioxide that has been produced by our cells (see pages 30-31).

NITROGEN – The human body does not require nitrogen, and as a result we exhale the same quantity as we inhale.

WATER – Water is another waste product produced by the cells and expelled through the lungs. Exhaled air contains more water than inhaled air. When you breathe outside on a cold winter day you can see the water vapour in your breath condense (turn from a gas into a liquid) in the air.

A CLOSER LOOK AT THE ALVEOLI

The alveoli are perfect for gaseous exchange for several reasons:

(1) Their walls are only one cell thick, which allows gases to cross them easily.

(2) Collectively they have a very large surface area across which gases can pass. In the average human's lungs, the total surface area is around 100 square metres.

(3) Each alveolus contains a net of tiny blood vessels called capillaries. The capillary walls are very thin. Oxygen and carbon dioxide can cross from the alveolus into the capillary, and vice versa, very easily.

▼ This cutaway diagram of the alveoli shows the path down which the air travels – through the bronchioles and into the alveoli air sacs.

ALVEOLI CROSS-SECTION

Oxygen in

Network of capillaries through which blood carries oxygen and carbon dioxide.

ENTERING THE BLOODSTREAM

Inhaled air in the alveoli is rich in oxygen. The blood in the capillaries is low in oxygen because it has come from the body where the oxygen is used up by the cells. This blood is now deoxygenated. Oxygen passes into the bloodstream by diffusion. Diffusion happens when there is a greater concentration of a substance in one area than in another. In this case, oxygen moves from an area rich in oxygen to an area that is less rich in oxygen. Oxygen is carried in the blood by a chemical called haemoglobin. Haemoglobin is found inside red blood cells.

The blood becomes oxygenated. It travels back to the heart where it is pumped to all of the cells of the body. When you exercise, most of the oxygenated blood is pumped to hard-working muscles, such as leg and arm muscles. If you have just eaten, the oxygenated blood will be used by the cells of the digestive system to help process food.

Respiring (working) cells release carbon dioxide into the bloodstream (see pages 30-31). The carbon-dioxide-rich blood is pumped to the lungs and the carbon dioxide passes into the alveoli by diffusion. The carbon dioxide is exhaled through the lungs.

OTHER SYSTEMS

Not all animals extract oxygen from the air. Fish extract dissolved oxygen from water using gills instead of lungs. When a fish opens and close its mouth it is gulping water in and across its gills. As the water passes over the gill surface, oxygen diffuses into the fish and carbon dioxide diffuses out in the same way as in humans. Some fish are ram ventilators. They swim very quickly, which makes more water pass across the gill surface to increase their gaseous exchange. Tuna fish are ram ventilators. They have high oxygen demands because they are large active fish. They must constantly swim at speeds of at least 65 centimetres per second or they will suffocate.

▲ A tuna fish must keep swimming in order to breathe.

LIVING WITH RESPIRATORY PROBLEMS

Not everyone has a healthy respiratory system. There are a number of relatively common conditions, such as asthma, with which people live and manage on a daily basis.

ASTHMA

It is likely that there is at least one person in your class who suffers from asthma. It is an increasingly common condition in the developed world. In the UK and USA, it affects eight per cent of adults and 11 per cent of children. Asthmatics have attacks of wheezing and shortness of breath. These attacks differ in their seriousness and duration and can usually be controlled with medication. Asthmatics can lead healthy and normal lives once their condition is diagnosed and controlled.

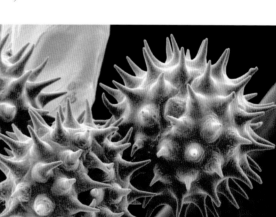

Normal windpipe

Inflamed windpipe

A sticky substance called mucus is present in our windpipes (trachea, bronchi and bronchioles). The windpipes are also lined with small hairs called cilia. The mucus traps germs that enter the windpipes and the cilia sweep it up to the trachea. When you cough, you bring the germs and mucus back to your mouth. The substance that you cough up is called phlegm. This is part of the body's natural **immunity** (protection against infection), but it can become overactive in asthmatics.

▲ In asthmatics, narrow, inflamed windpipes reduce the amount of oxygen reaching the alveoli.

WHAT IS AN ASTHMA ATTACK?

During an asthma attack, the muscles of the bronchi contract, which narrows the windpipe and makes breathing difficult. The lining of the windpipe becomes irritated and swollen and produces excess mucus. The extra mucus can block the smaller bronchioles of the respiratory system and cause further breathing difficulties.

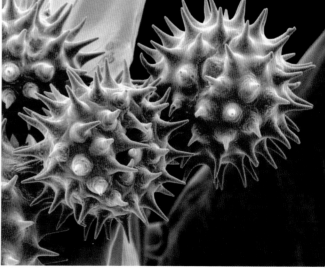

WHAT CAUSES AN ASTHMA ATTACK?

Some people have an **allergic reaction** when they come into contact with a particular substance, such as pollen, animal fur or dust mites. Asthmatics may have an asthma attack when they are exposed to a substance to which they are allergic. Others may have an attack if they exercise too hard or breathe in very cold air. Asthmatics may be

▲ Pollen from flowers can trigger an asthma attack in some people.

especially vulnerable to an attack if they have a cold or infection of the respiratory system, or if they are under a lot of stress.

HOW IS ASTHMA MONITORED AND TREATED?

Doctors can measure the severity of asthma using a peak flow meter. When you blow into the meter, it calculates how many litres of air you exhale per minute. The peak flow reading is lower in an asthmatic than in someone with a healthy respiratory system. Peak flow meters are used to decide whether asthma treatments are improving the individual's respiratory health. Asthma medicines are usually given through an inhaler. Inhalers are useful because the drugs are taken directly into the lungs, which can quickly reduce the symptoms. The medicines relax the muscles of the windpipes and allow more air to pass through them. They also reduce the inflammation in the windpipes.

Non-drug treatments can also reduce the symptoms of some asthmatics, although there has been very little scientific research on such complementary therapies. Breathing exercises that alter the amount of oxygen and carbon dioxide in exhaled air may help return breathing patterns to that of someone with a healthy respiratory system. Yoga also includes breathing exercises, and is designed to reduce stress, which may make an asthma attack less likely.

▲ Some people believe that yoga and breathing exercises can help asthmatics.

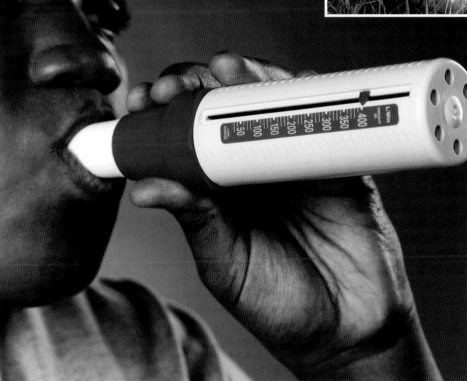

◀ By measuring the quantity of air exhaled through a peak flow meter, a doctor can assess a patient's respiratory health.

Respiration and energy

Respiration and breathing are not the same. The purpose of breathing is to provide our cells with oxygen for use in respiration. Respiration is the process of using oxygen to release the energy in the food that we eat. Each of our cells contains tiny structures called **mitochondria**. This is where respiration takes place. There are many mitochondria in cells that carry out a lot of respiration, such as leg muscle cells, and few mitochondria in less active parts of the body, such as skin cells.

TYPES OF RESPIRATION

Respiration can occur in two ways depending on how much oxygen is available.

(1) Aerobic respiration – releasing energy with oxygen.

(2) Anaerobic respiration – releasing energy without oxygen.

AEROBIC RESPIRATION

When you imagine a chemical reaction that releases energy, you are likely to think of lots of fire and flames. During such combustion reactions, a fuel is burned in oxygen to release energy in the form of heat and fire. In our bodies, a similar process occurs, but thankfully without the flames! The fuel for respiration is the food that we eat. The oxygen allows the reaction to proceed and the energy is released in chemical form.

This reaction represents aerobic respiration:

Glucose + Oxygen ➡
Carbon Dioxide + Water + Energy

Aerobic respiration releases around 15 kilojoules of energy for every gram of glucose that is respired. The waste products are water and carbon dioxide. The energy is stored for later use or used for life processes, such as growth and movement.

ANAEROBIC RESPIRATION

Glucose can also be broken down without the presence of oxygen. This was important for early life on Earth because thousands of millions of years ago there was little oxygen in the atmosphere. The ancient bacteria had to survive through anaerobic respiration.

This reaction represents anaerobic respiration:

Glucose ➡ Lactate + Energy

▲ Food is the fuel used for respiration inside our cells.

This process is a lot less efficient than aerobic respiration. It releases only 0.83 kilojoules of energy for every gram of glucose that is respired. Lactate is the waste product. You may have experienced a cramp in your muscles when you exercise. This happens when you do not have enough oxygen to respire aerobically. You then respire anaerobically and lactic acid builds up in your muscles causing cramp.

LONG- AND SHORT-DISTANCE RUNNING

Long-distance runners mainly respire aerobically. The runner gets into a rhythm and can maintain a steady pace over a period of hours. The heart and lungs can supply enough oxygen to the muscles, which allows the runner to keep going.

Sprinters mainly respire anaerobically during short races. Their heart and lungs cannot take in oxygen quickly enough to meet the demands of their muscles. Once the race is complete, the lactic acid that has built up in the muscles is gradually removed as oxygen is taken in and the body returns to aerobic respiration.

▲ Short-distance runners do not rely on oxygen for their energy. For a short period of time, they respire anaerobically.

DID YOU KNOW?

▶ Long distance runners often train at high altitudes (right) where the pressure of oxygen in the atmosphere is much lower than at sea level. Scientists believe that training at such heights means that the athletes learn to take longer and more efficient breaths.

▶ Scientists believe that billions of years ago, mitochondria were organisms that lived inside bacteria. They helped the bacteria to respire aerobically. Eventually, the mitochondria became so dependent on the bacteria that they lost all of their other life processes. Today, the mitochondria inside humans are no longer organisms, they are organelles (tiny organs).

Smoking, alcohol and drugs

Health is defined as 'an absence of disease'. To keep your body and mind healthy, it is important to follow a balanced diet, exercise regularly and have plenty of sleep. However, many of us often do not follow these recommendations. For example, you may eat a lot of fatty or sugary food even though you know it can lead to medical problems such as obesity or heart disease. The same could be said for smoking tobacco and drinking alcohol. We know they are bad for the human body, yet people all over the world continue to smoke and drink.

SMOKING

Cigarettes contain hundreds of ingredients, many of which are harmful to the human body. Over 4,000 chemicals are created when cigarettes are burned, and 43 of these are known carcinogens (chemicals that cause cancer). One of the most significant ingredients in cigarette smoke is nicotine. This is the chemical that causes the smoker to become 'addicted' and is the main reason that people continue to smoke.

Smokers get a sense of physical well-being from cigarettes as the chemicals travel around their bodies. Their heart rate and blood pressure rise, which causes them to feel more alert. They may also feel calmer even though their bodies are not calming down at all.

▼ The lung on the left is from a non-smoker. The lung on the right is from a smoker. It has been damaged by tar, nicotine and other chemicals found in cigarette smoke.

THE HARMFUL INGREDIENTS IN CIGARETTES

Ingredients	Damaging effects	What happens?
Tar	Bronchitis (infection of the bronchioles) and emphysema	Tar stops the cilia in the trachea from beating. Mucus and bacteria cannot be properly removed. Bacteria can enter the lungs and cause bronchitis. A forceful cough may develop, which can damage the precious alveoli. Eventually, the smoker becomes breathless and may have to breathe oxygen from a tank. This condition is called emphysema and cannot be reversed.
Carbon monoxide	Carbon monoxide poisoning	Carbon monoxide enters the bloodstream and binds with haemoglobin in the red blood cells. Haemoglobin normally carries oxygen around the body in the blood. The haemoglobin is then unable to collect oxygen and the smoker becomes breathless.
Smoke particles, ammonia and sulphur dioxide	Smoker's cough	These ingredients are irritating to the windpipes and cause a smoker to cough regularly. This can also damage the alveoli.

Amongst other conditions, smoking also contributes to the ageing of skin cells (wrinkles), cancer of the mouth, larynx (voice box) and lungs, high blood pressure, heart disease, low sperm count in men, lowered fertility in women and a higher rate of miscarriage, asthma, pneumonia, gum disease and leukaemia.

There are many organisations committed to encouraging young people not to take up smoking in the first place, and helping people to quit. In many parts of the world, smoking is banned in places of work and on public transport. In some places, such as the UK, and parts of the USA and Australia, smoking is banned in all public places.

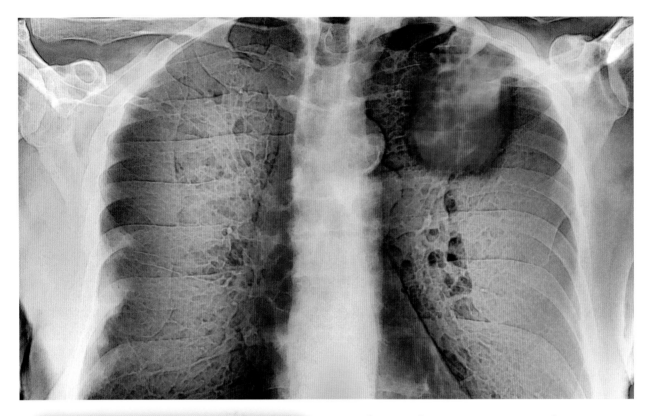

▲ This x-ray shows a cancerous tumour (orange, top right) in the lungs. If the cancer has not spread, it may be removed surgically. Other treatments include chemotherapy and radiotherapy.

DID YOU KNOW?

▶ Non-smokers who breathe other people's smoke are also at risk of the same problems as smokers. This is called 'passive smoking'. When people are exposed to passive smoking over a long period of time, they are between 10 and 30 per cent more likely to develop lung cancer than people who don't breathe in any smoke. Because of passive smoking, each year in the USA, 3,000 non-smokers die from lung cancer.

▶ A study carried out by British scientists found that smoking decreases life expectancy by 10 years. They also found out that almost half of the smokers in the study died from smoking-related illness.

TEST YOURSELF

▶ How do you think smoking can make you unattractive to other people?

▶ How would you try to convince someone to stop smoking?

▶ Smokers find it very difficult to quit smoking. Name three products that are available to aid this process.

ALCOHOL

In many parts of the world, drinking alcohol is an accepted social practice. Alcoholic drinks are easily bought if you are over the legal age. Many people enjoy drinking alcohol across the world without any ill effects. Unfortunately, when drunk in large amounts, alcohol can be addictive and lead to life-threatening disease.

▼ Drinking in moderation can be safe, but excessive, prolonged or binge drinking can have serious short and long term side-effects.

EFFECTS OF DRINKING ALCOHOL
ON BEHAVIOUR

Alcohol is a depressant, which means that it slows down brain activity. Alcohol makes some people feel relaxed and less inhibited, which can make them louder and more confident. However, alcohol can also cause people to become argumentative and aggressive. Continued alcohol use can lead to depression.

Alcohol is measured in units. In the UK, one unit is equal to half a pint of standard beer, one small glass of wine or one 25 millilitre measure of spirits. The number of units of alcohol consumed determines the effects on an individual. The more alcohol consumed, the stronger and potentially more dangerous the effects.

Unit size and government recommendations vary from country to country. This table shows the recommendations for a small selection of countries:

Country	Amount of alcohol per unit	One unit equals (approximately)	Government recommendations
Australia	13 millilitres	$2/3$ of a pint of beer	No more than 14 units per week for women and 28 units for men.
Japan	25 millilitres	1 and $1/4$ pints of beer	No more than one or two units per day
UK	10 millilitres	$1/2$ pint of beer	No more than 14 units per week for women and 21 units for men
USA	18 millilitres	1 pint of beer	No more than 7 units per week for women and 14 units for men

DID YOU KNOW?

▶ Scientists have found a chemical in mice that may control alcohol consumption. When alcohol is given to mice who do not have this chemical, they over-indulge in alcohol. The presence or absence of this chemical in humans may explain why some people pursue heavy drinking whilst others only drink moderately. Perhaps in the future, scientists will develop a version of this chemical to treat alcoholism.

MEDICAL EFFECTS OF DRINKING ALCOHOL

Alcohol is absorbed through the stomach wall, and through the small intestine. It reaches the bloodstream and travels to the brain very quickly. As the concentration of alcohol in the bloodstream builds up, it slows reaction times and reduces the ability to control movement and speech. Therefore, many people are injured while drunk. For example, in one study, 43 per cent of teenagers admitted with injuries to a hospital in the USA tested positive for alcohol. If the blood alcohol concentration reaches dangerous levels, it causes nausea and vomiting, coma and eventually death.

Alcoholics are addicted to and regularly drink large amounts of alcohol. In most cases alcoholics are unable to stop their destructive drinking without medical help. The liver is the organ that removes alcohol from the bloodstream. Over a long period of time, the liver is damaged by the alcohol and the alcoholic is likely to suffer from cirrhosis of the liver. This condition stops the liver from working properly and cannot be reversed. Long-term alcohol abuse can also lead to brain damage, heart failure, an inflamed stomach and liver failure. Similar medical problems can also happen to non-addicts who regularly drink large amounts of alcohol. This is commonly known as binge drinking.

ILLEGAL DRUGS

Illegal drugs, such as cannabis, ecstasy and cocaine, are taken by people for their mood-altering effects. Some people take drugs to fit in with their friends. However, many drugs are addictive and some can have permanent or fatal side-effects. Drugs that are quickly addictive, such as heroin and cocaine, are called **hard drugs**, whereas those that are less addictive, such as marijuana, are called **soft drugs**.

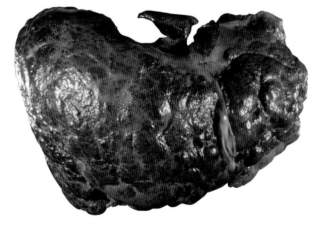

▼ This liver's surface is scarred where parts of the liver have died. Liver cirrhosis (damage) like this can be caused by drinking too much alcohol over a long period of time.

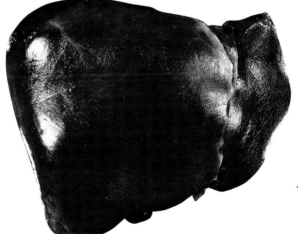

INVESTIGATE

▶ Use library books and the internet to find out what binge drinking is and why it is so bad for the human body. Write a short summary to explain your findings.

◀ This healthy liver is smooth.

Infection and disease

It is normal for us to become unwell from time to time. At some point, you are likely to have had an illness, such as a cold, chicken pox or a stomach upset. Often we become unwell when our bodies are attacked by a **pathogen**. A pathogen is a foreign body, such as a bacterium or a virus, that causes disease. Many pathogens are easily spread from one person to another; they are referred to as infectious.

TYPES OF PATHOGEN

When pathogens enter our bodies, they take nutrients from us, divide within us and can also secrete poisons. It is these actions that cause us to feel unwell. Viruses, bacteria, fungi, protists and worms can act as pathogens.

VIRAL INFECTION

Viruses are microorganisms – they are so small that you need a microscope to see them. They enter human cells (host cells) and make the cell into a virus-producing machine. When the host cell cannot contain the numerous viruses anymore, they are released and go on to infect more cells. The common cold and influenza are both caused by viruses.

Because viruses live within our cells, treatment is very difficult. To destroy the virus, you have to destroy the host cell. This is not an option with most viruses. Therefore, the common cold and influenza are dealt with by the individual's **immune system** (see page 39). It can take between three days and several weeks for the immune system to get rid of the cold or 'flu virus.

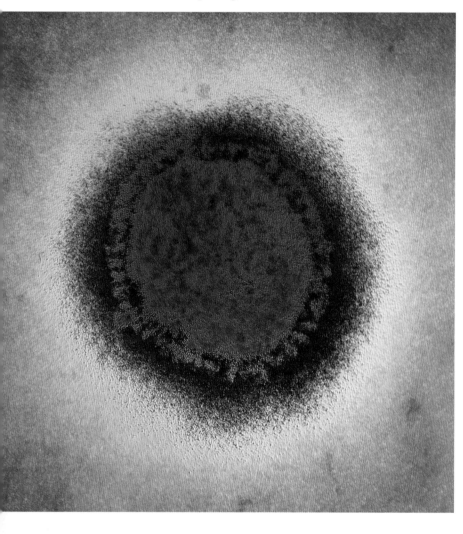

◀ This is an influenza virus. The spikes that surround its central body stick to the host's cells. Once infected, the host will suffer the symptoms of influenza. The virus is about 100 nanometres in diameter (0.0001 millimetres).

BACTERIAL INFECTION

Bacteria are also microorganisms. Some bacteria are very useful. For example, bacteria are used to make cheese and beer. However, other bacteria can cause illness when they enter the human body. Bacteria reproduce very rapidly and their numbers can quickly become unmanageable. Bacteria cause cholera, whooping cough, food poisoning and tuberculosis.

Bacteria affect the body in many different ways. For example, dental bacteria release acid as they feed on sugar found on our teeth. The acid burns away at the enamel on the surface of our teeth and causes tooth decay. Other bacteria release harmful substances into our bloodstreams. Some bacteria actually attack and destroy our cells. The good news is that many bacterial infections are easily treated using **antibiotics**.

FUNGAL, PROTIST AND WORM INFECTIONS

Amongst other conditions, fungi can cause athlete's foot. The fungi grow and reproduce in the moist gaps between the toes. They release enzymes, which digest (eat) the skin surface.

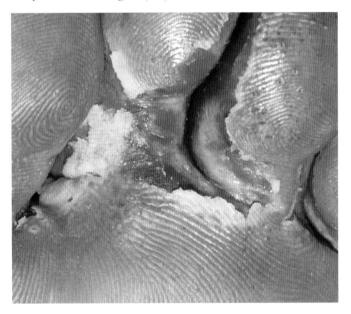

▲ Athlete's foot is a common fungal infection.

Protists are also microorganisms. One type of protist, called plasmodium, lives inside mosquitoes. When the infected mosquitoes bite humans they can cause malaria. Malaria is one of the planet's deadliest diseases and kills up to 2.7 million people each year, mainly in developing countries.

▲ Mosquitoes breed in still or stagnant water.

Tapeworms can live in the guts of many animals, including humans. Tapeworms feed on the nutrients that the animal has consumed. Symptoms include a large appetite with no weight gain. Tapeworms can reproduce and make their way to other parts of the body, such as the liver and the eyes. This can be very serious.

▼ Tapeworms cling onto the insides of the host's intestine using hooks and circular suckers. Tapeworms can grow up to 60 centimetres long.

SPREADING DISEASE

Infectious diseases are spread in a number of ways. Many can be avoided through good hygiene and care with what we eat and drink. The exposure to some disease-causing bacteria can be good for us as it tests our bodies and builds up our immunity. Those that live in a very sterile environment can often be made the most ill.

DID YOU KNOW?

▶ Bacteria can adapt to antibiotics so that the medicine is no longer effective against them. When treated with a course of antibiotics, a bacteria population is usually eliminated. If a course of antibiotics is not completed, a few bacteria may survive. These are the strongest members of the population. Bacteria can reproduce in 20 minutes, which means that the strong bacteria could form a new population very rapidly. This population will be resistant to the antibiotic and are known as 'superbugs'. It is important to always complete a course of antibiotics so that superbugs do not develop.

This table shows the main ways in which infection can spread:

Disease example	Method of spreading disease	Preventing the disease
Cholera (The bacteria that cause cholera can live in water.)	Water	Always drink clean water. In some countries, it is best to drink bottled or filtered water.
Athlete's foot (Caused by a fungus)	Direct contact	Avoid touching an infected area on another person or on yourself. Some bacteria and viruses can enter through cuts in the skin or though the mouth – always wash your hands after going to the toilet.
Malaria (Caused by a protist)	Insects (Other animals can pass on different diseases)	Avoid being bitten by insects, for example, by using an insect repellent and wearing long sleeves. Wash food that may have been in contact with animals.
Influenza and the common cold (Both caused by viruses)	Air	Use a tissue when sneezing and avoid coming into close and confined contact with anyone who is infected.
Salmonella (bacteria) and tapeworm	Food	Ensure food has not passed its 'use by' date. Food must be cooked properly to kill microorganisms.

PREVENTING PATHOGEN ENTRY

Our bodies are well designed to prevent attack from pathogens. Often we are not even aware of the attack.

The human body's physical barriers to pathogens include:

(1) **Eyes** – Blinking cleans the eyes and prevents pathogen entry. The eyes are also washed clean by tears.

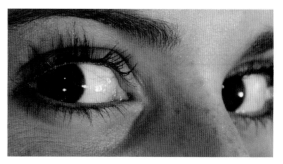

▲ Blinking protects the eye. Tears are a mild antiseptic.

(2) Stomach – Stomach acid kills most pathogens that have been accidentally eaten. In some cases the stomach gets rid of harmful pathogens by vomiting.

(3) Skin – The skin is a relatively thick layer that is difficult to penetrate. The surface of the skin is a dead layer of cells through which it is impossible for germs to enter. Skin in the nose and ears contains hairs and mucus, which also helps prevent pathogen entry. When the skin is cut, pathogens can enter the bloodstream. To prevent this, platelets in the blood seal up the cut by forming a blood clot. A scab quickly forms. New skin grows under the scab, which eventually falls off.

(4) Lungs – The trachea and bronchioles are lined with fine cilia and mucus secreting cells. Together these trap pathogens that have been breathed in and expel them again by coughing.

THE IMMUNE SYSTEM

Despite our best efforts, pathogens can still enter our bodies and cause illness. When this happens, our bodies launch an **immune response**, which fights the pathogen. This battle can often make us feel unwell until the attack is under control.

White blood cells produce proteins called antibodies. Antibodies stick to the pathogen, which makes it easier for your body to destroy them. Antibodies remain in the bloodstream so that a future attack by the same pathogen can be swiftly dealt with.

WHAT HAPPENS WHEN YOU CUT YOURSELF?

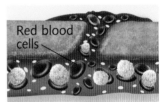
Red blood cells

◀ Blood escapes from the wound. White blood cells and platelets collect at the wound site.

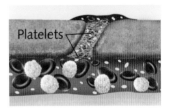
Platelets

◀ The platelets help the blood to clot which stops the bleeding. White blood cells fight any pathogens that may have entered the body.

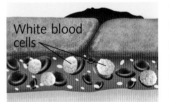
White blood cells

◀ A scab forms which seals the wound and prevents further pathogen entry. The tissue re-grows underneath the scab.

TEST YOURSELF

▶ Next time you have a small cut, try to notice the stages of your immune response. Write an account of what happens and how long each stage of repair lasts.

◀ This photograph shows the turbulence in the air caused by a sneeze. A sneeze can propel mucus and cold-causing viruses at 167 km/hr over a distance of five metres.

HIV

One disease that attacks the immune system is Acquired Immune Deficiency Syndrome (AIDS). AIDS is caused by the Human Immunodeficiency Virus (HIV).

WHAT ARE HIV AND AIDS?

In 1979, doctors in New York and Los Angeles in the USA reported rare types of pneumonia, cancer and other illnesses that were not usually seen in people with healthy immune systems. This information was reported to the Centres for Disease Control and Prevention (CDC), the branch of the US government that monitors and attempts to control disease outbreaks. In 1982, the CDC named the condition AIDS, and in 1984, the virus responsible for weakening the immune system was identified as HIV. HIV is believed to have originated in primates in Africa, and then become able to infect humans.

Following HIV infection, it can take around 10 years or more for AIDS to develop. AIDS cripples the immune system by destroying cells that are designed to help the body fight infection. Patients eventually die from secondary infections such as pneumonia.

WHO HAS HIV?

Both men and women, whether they are heterosexual or homosexual, can contract HIV and develop AIDS. The total number of AIDS deaths globally between 1981 and the end of 2003 was 20 million. By 2007, nearly 33 million people globally were estimated to be living with HIV. In 2007 alone, AIDS killed two million people and 2.7 million people became infected with HIV.

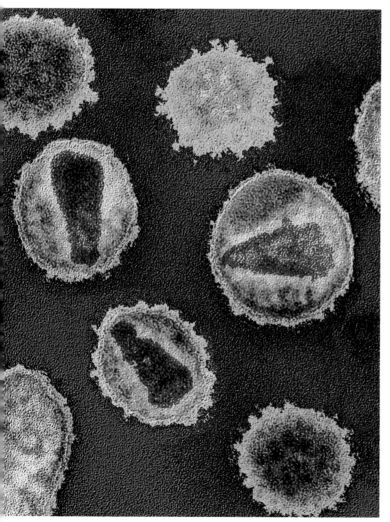

▲ The HIV virus kills the host's immune response cells.

▲ Vigils are carried out across the world to remember the victims of AIDS and to promote understanding of the disease.

TOTAL NEW AIDS INFECTIONS BETWEEN 1999 AND 2002

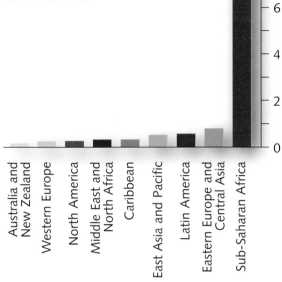

▼ This graph shows that the total number of new infections is massively greater in Sub-Saharan Africa than anywhere else in the world.

Millions of people

14
12
10
8
6
4
2
0

Australia and New Zealand
Western Europe
North America
Middle East and North Africa
Caribbean
East Asia and Pacific
Latin America
Eastern Europe and Central Asia
Sub-Saharan Africa

HOW IS HIV SPREAD?

HIV can only be transmitted through body fluids such as blood, semen, vaginal secretions, from mother to baby across the placenta, and through breast milk. The most common form of transmission is through sexual intercourse. Condoms act as a physical barrier and prevent HIV from spreading. HIV can also be transmitted through blood and organ transfers, although in most countries, hospitals routinely check for the virus. HIV is also spread through sharing contaminated hypodermic needles. Touching or sharing towels, clothes or toilets can not transmit HIV.

DIAGNOSIS AND TREATMENT

HIV is diagnosed through a blood test, which looks for antibodies against the virus. If the test is positive, patients are often referred to specialist centres for monitoring, treatment and counselling. Although there is no cure for HIV, medication can effectively slow its progress. However, the medication often has side effects. Some side-effects are relatively mild, such as gas and bloating, and dry skin. Others are much more serious, such as kidney problems, brittle bones and nerve damage. Once full-blown AIDS has developed, medication is used to fight any infections and extend the life of the patient. In poorer parts of the world, people are more vulnerable to becoming infected with HIV because they have less access to information, education, health care services and means of prevention. Once infected, they cannot afford the expensive anti-HIV medication. Unfortunately, these are often the areas where HIV infection is widespread. Sub-Saharan Africa, for example, is home to 10 per cent of the world's population, but is home to 65 per cent of the world's population infected with HIV – over 25 million people. Organisations such as the World Health Organisation (WHO) are working hard to get anti-HIV medication to these areas.

▼ Sub-Saharan Africa has been hardest hit by the HIV virus.

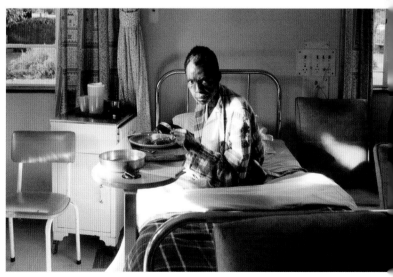

Although our immune systems protect us well against pathogens, sometimes the human body needs a little extra help. Vaccinations are used to strengthen the immune system and increase life expectancy. Vaccinations involve injecting an individual with a small dose of a particular disease or pathogen. The dose is not large enough to cause the illness to develop, but the body begins to create antibodies against the disease. The antibodies remain in the bloodstream so that if the pathogen returns, the immune system is prepared to fight it effectively. Edward Jenner discovered the principal behind vaccinations in the late 1700s.

THE FATHER OF VACCINATION

Edward Jenner was born in 1749 in the UK. At the age of 14, Jenner became an apprentice to a surgeon, Dr Daniel Ludlow. He moved to London in 1770 to begin work as a surgeon in St. George's Hospital. He studied under the famous surgeon John Hunter. Dr Hunter became aware of Jenner's observational and investigation skills. When he was 23 years old, Jenner returned to his childhood village of Berkeley and became the town doctor and surgeon.

▲ Edward Jenner's discoveries changed medicine forever and saved countless lives.

SMALLPOX

During the 1700s a disease called smallpox was rife across the world. Smallpox causes fever, nausea, vomiting, back- and head-ache, severe abdominal pain, pus filled sores and often death. Those who survived suffered terrible scarring.

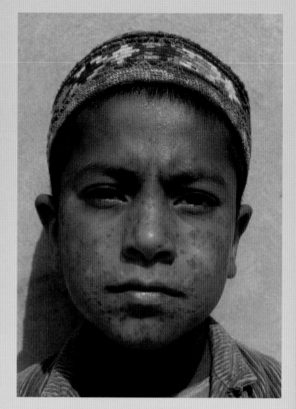

▲ This smallpox scarring occurred around 1970, before smallpox was eliminated from the planet.

At the time, it was common knowledge that anyone who survived smallpox became immune to the disease (they would not catch it again). Therefore, medical experts tried to prevent smallpox by injecting healthy people with a mild dose of the disease.

This resulted in three problems:

(1) The disease did not always remain mild, and healthy people died.
(2) The person who received the mild dose was able to pass the disease on to others.
(3) It rarely gave permanent immunity to smallpox.

Edward Jenner noticed that people who worked with cattle had a much lower incidence of smallpox. Jenner wondered whether this was because they were constantly exposed to cowpox, which was a relatively harmless disease. Cowpox caused a few days of discomfort and some small pocks (pus-filled blisters).

▲ This drawing of the pocks caused by cowpox is from a book by Edward Jenner published in 1798.

In 1796, Jenner rubbed pus from the milkmaid's cowpox sores into scratches on the arm of an eight-year-old boy. As expected, the boy contracted cowpox, but after six weeks he made a full recovery. Then came the ultimate test – Jenner exposed the boy to smallpox. To everyone's relief, the boy did not develop the disease. He had become immune to smallpox. Today we know that the viruses that cause cowpox and smallpox are very similar. Therefore, exposure to cowpox causes the human body to produce antibodies that also work against smallpox.

To further prove his theory, Jenner repeated the experiment on his own son. Again, the immunisation was successful. He called his method 'vaccination'. In 1798, Jenner published his results in a medical journal and in the 1800s, wide-scale vaccination began. Global vaccination meant that smallpox was eliminated from our planet by 1977.

▼ This engraving was done by Sol Eytinge in 1873. It shows smallpox vaccination of the poor.

VACCINATIONS TODAY

In many parts of the world, vaccinations are routinely offered to children and adults to combat a large number of diseases. Some diseases, such as tuberculosis, only require one vaccination and the antibodies generated remain in the body for life. Others last a number of months or years and successive vaccinations are required to make sure the immunity lasts.

CHILDHOOD VACCINATIONS

In many countries, the following vaccinations are recommended for children.

Age	Vaccinations
Between two and four months old	Diptheria, tetanus, polio, meningitis C
13 months	Measles, mumps and rubella (MMR)
Between three and five years old	Diptheria, tetanus, polio, Measles, mumps and rubella (MMR)
Between 10 and 14 years old	BCG (against tuberculosis) – not always needed so a skin test is carried out first.
Between 13 and 18 years old	Diptheria, tetanus, polio

ADULT VACCINATIONS

Tetanus boosters are given to people who are at risk of contracting tetanus following an injury. Polio boosters are advised every 10 years for healthcare workers who may be exposed to the disease. Flu and pneumonia vaccines are offered to people with weaker immune systems, such as the elderly. Hepatitis B vaccine is offered to people who may come into contact with the disease, such as healthcare workers.

THE MMR DEBATE

Some vaccinations contain more than one vaccine. Some believe that vaccinating against several diseases at once places too much stress on the body. One combined vaccination, called MMR (measles, mumps and rubella), is given as part of some childhood vaccination programmes. Each of these diseases, if contracted, has serious complications:

Measles – This causes a range of symptoms from ear infection and bronchitis to convulsions (fits) or brain damage, and can be fatal.

Mumps – This causes swelling in the face, fever, headache, sore throat, temporary deafness, inflammation of the pancreas, and pain and swelling in the testicles in older males.

▼ Measles lasts around a week. Although it can be free from complications, one out of 1,000 people with measles dies from the illness.

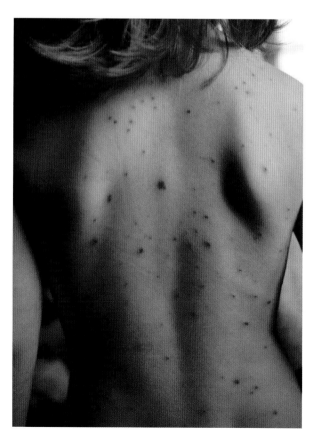

Rubella – In young people, this causes a rash. However, it can lead to painful joints, blood disorders and swelling of the brain. It is particularly dangerous if caught by a pregnant woman as it can cause serious damage to the unborn baby. The baby may be born with some deafness, blindness, and a damaged heart or brain.

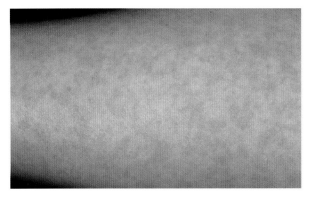

▲ Rubella is usually mild and highly contagious. The rash lasts for around three days.

There has been some controversy about the MMR vaccine in recent years, owing to a study published in a medical journal in 1998 by Dr Andrew Wakefield. His initial study appeared to show a link between the MMR vaccine and a condition called autism. Autism affects the brain's development. Autism sufferers have problems with their social and communication skills.

However, further studies have been unable to prove any association between MMR and autism. Medical experts in the UK promote the triple vaccination, although some parents pay privately for three individual vaccinations. It is dangerous for a child to not be fully vaccinated against these three diseases.

▶ On average, only half the children in sub-Saharan Africa are immunised fully. The world average is 77 per cent.

GLOBAL VACCINATION

Vaccination programmes vary across the world for a number of different reasons. These include: (1) the cost of medication, (2) the standard of healthcare that is available in the country, and (3) the likelihood of coming into contact with particular pathogens.

An initiative launched in 2000 is making vaccinations available to children across 75 of the world's poorest countries. The Global Alliance for Vaccines and Immunisation (GAVI) is administering the project, which was kick-started by a $750m contribution from Microsoft founder, Bill Gates. Amongst other achievements, by 2008 GAVI had immunised over 190 million children against the hepatitis B virus. Since 2005, one type of meningitis has been almost eliminated in The Gambia.

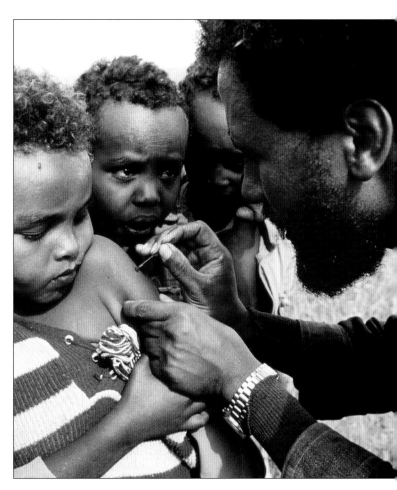

Glossary

ADOLESCENCE – The stage of growth and development which occurs between the ages of 10 and 15, during which a child turns into an adult.

ALLERGIC REACTION – An over-reaction of the body's defence system to a foreign body.

ANTIBIOTICS – Substances that kill bacteria.

ANTIBODIES – Proteins that tag, or stick to pathogens to help the body recognise and destroy them.

CONCEPTION – The point at which a sperm fertilises an ovum.

COPULATION – Sexual intercourse.

DIFFUSION – This is where a substance moves from an area where it is in high concentration to one where it is in low concentration.

EJACULATION – The ejection of sperm from the penis.

FERTILISATION – The fusion of a sperm and an ovum.

GAMETES – The sex cells. Sperm and eggs are gametes. They contain half of the information necessary to create a new individual.

GASEOUS EXCHANGE – In humans this is the process by which oxygen enters the bloodstream, and carbon dioxide is removed.

GROWTH SPURT – A sudden acceleration in the growth rate of an individual.

HARD DRUGS – Drugs that are believed to be more addictive, dangerous or harmful to the user, such as cocaine or heroin, than so-called soft drugs.

HORMONES – A chemical messenger found in the body. Hormones are produced in one part of the body and transferred to another part of the body, usually via the blood. They have a variety of different effects, depending on the type of hormone.

HUMAN GROWTH HORMONE – A chemical messenger produced in the brain that causes the tissues and organs of the body to grow.

IMMUNE RESPONSE – A reaction of the body to any substance that it recognises as foreign. The

---

ANSWERS

p9 Test yourself

A growth spurt is a rapid increase in height and weight that occurs before birth, during infancy and in adolescence.

Male secondary sexual characteristics:
Under arm, chest and pubic hair
Facial hair
Deepening of the voice
Broader shoulders and chest
Muscle development
A more obvious Adam's apple

Female secondary sexual characteristics:
Development of the breasts
Under arm and pubic hair growth
Widening of the hips
Development of fat deposits around the buttocks, thighs and hips

p11 Test yourself

A sperm cell leaves one of the testes, passes through the epididymis and along the sperm duct. It passes by the openings of the seminal vesicle, prostate gland and Cowper's gland as it travels through the urethra. It then carries on in the urethra through the penis and if sexual intercourse is taking place, it enters the female body.

p17 Test yourself

(1) Erection
(2) Copulation
(3) Ejaculation and orgasm
(4) Fertilisation
(5) Conception

p25 Investigate

When the rubber sheet is pulled down, the volume of the bell jar apparatus increases. This causes the pressure inside the jar to be lower than outside the jar. As a consequence, air rushes into the balloons and they inflate. When the rubber sheet is pushed up, the volume inside the bell jar apparatus decreases. The air pressure inside the jar increases which flattens the balloons.

The bell jar represents the rib cage, the rubber sheet represents the diaphragm and the balloons represent the lungs.

The bell jar is rigid, but in reality the rib cage can expand and contract a little.

response aims to neutralise the substance and restore health to the individual.

IMMUNE SYSTEM – The system of organs and cells that causes the immune response.

IMMUNITY – The ability of an organism to resist disease or infection.

MENSTRUATION – The shedding of the lining and blood from the uterus. This lasts between five and seven days and occurs roughly on a monthly basis.

MITOCHONDRIA – Organelles which produce energy for the cell. They turn food into energy during the process of respiration.

OXYGENATED – This is when a substance, such as blood, contains oxygen.

PATHOGEN – Any substance that is capable of causing disease. The term pathogen usually refers to a microorganism.

PRIMARY SEXUAL CHARACTERISTICS – The sex organs. In males these are the penis, testes, scrotum, prostate, seminal vesicles, epididymis, and Cowper's glands. In females, these are the vagina, vulva, cervix, uterus, oviducts (Fallopian tubes), ovaries and related glands.

PUBERTY – This is when the sex organs begin to work and an individual is capable of sexual reproduction.

SECONDARY SEXUAL CHARACTERISTICS – In males and females this is the development of body hair, such as under the arms, on the face and in the pubic region. In males the voice also deepens and muscles develop. In females, the breasts develop and the hips widen.

SEMEN – The combination of sperm, seminal fluid, and other male reproductive secretions.

SOFT DRUGS – Drugs that are considered to be less harmful than 'hard drugs'. These drugs are generally not physically addictive.

TRIMESTERS – Each three-month period in a nine month pregnancy.

Useful websites:
www.nationalgeographic.com
www.bbc.co.uk/schools
www.howstuffworks.com
www.newscientist.com
www.sciencenewsforkids.org

p33 Test yourself
Smoking can make you unattractive to other people by causing your breath, clothes and hair to smell, your teeth and fingers are likely to become stained with tar.

To convince someone to stop smoking you could tell them that they are paying for a habit that is likely to kill them or cause them serious illness in the future.

Products that are available to help people give up smoking include nicotine patches, nicotine chewing gum and nicotine inhalers.

p35 Investigate
Binge drinking is commonly defined as consuming between five and 11 drinks on one occasion for the sole purpose of becoming intoxicated. However, this does depend on social setting, the types of drink consumed, the time period over which they are consumed and perhaps even the drinker's age and body size.

It is bad for the human body because it can cause vomiting, unconsciousness, slow or irregular breathing and even death. Over a longer period it can seriously damage the liver. Binge drinking is also associated with injuries.

p39 Test yourself
The wound bled for two minutes. The area around it turned red and sore for four days. It was red because blood collects in the area to repair the skin. It also looked a bit swollen because white blood cells gather at the site as part of the immune response. The immune response kills any pathogens. The scab started to appear within 24 hours and then hardened over the next few days. The scab formed because the platelets in the blood produced a protective mesh over the wound preventing further infection, which then hardened. The scab fell off after about a week. It left a reddened site and a tiny scar. The scar formed because the new skin did not look exactly the same as the skin that was there before.

Index

Page references in italics
represent pictures.

PHOTO CREDITS – *(abbv: r, right, l, left, t, top, m, middle, b, bottom)* **Front cover images** Fotolia **p.1** (t) Martina Misar/www.istockphoto.com (bl) Ana Abejon/www.istockphoto.com **p.2** Peter Scoones/Science Photo Library **p.3** (b) Susumu Nishinaga/Science Photo Library **p.4** (tl) Krzysztof Chrystowski/www.istockphoto.com (br) Eye of Science/Science Photo Library **p.5** Eye of Science/Science Photo Library **p.6** (t) Andrei Tchernov/www.istockphoto.com (b) Scott Camazine/Science Photo Library **p.8** Science Photo Library **p.15** Professor P.M. Motta, G. Macchiarelli, S.A., Nottola/Science Photo Library **p.16** Ana Abejon/www.istockphoto.com **p.17** Eye of Science/Science Photo Library **p.18** (t) Steve Gschmeissner/Science Photo Library (b) Scimat/Science Photo Library **p.19** (t) John McLean/Science Photo Library (m) Zephyr/Science Photo Library (b) Pascal Goetgheluck **p.20** (t) Gary Parker/Science Photo Library (bl) Paige Foster/www.istockphoto.com (br) Scott Camazine/Sue Trainor/Science Photo Library **p.21** Matthew Bowden/www.istockphoto.com **p.27** Peter Scoones/Science Photo Library **p.28** Susumu Nishinaga/Science Photo Library **p.29** (t) Krzysztof Chrystowski/www.istockphoto.com (b) Coneyl Jay/Science Photo Library **p.30** Martina Misar/www.istockphoto.com **p.31** (b) Duomo/CORBIS (b) A. Glauberman/Science Photo Library **p.33** Du Cane Medical Imaging Ltd/Science Photo Library **p.34** www.istockphoto.com **p.35** (l) CNRI/Science Photo Library (r) CNRI/Science Photo Library **p.36** NIBSC/Science Photo Library **p.37** (t) R. Umesh Chandran, TDR, WHO/Science Photo Library (bl) Science Photo Library (br) Eye of Science/Science Photo Library **p.38** Matthew Gough/www.istockphoto.com **p.39** Dr Gary Settles/Science Photo Library **p.40** (l) Eye of Science/Science Photo Library (r) John Cole/Science Photo Library **p.41** Chris Sattlberger/Science Photo Library **p.42** (tr) Paul Almasy/CORBIS (bl) Jean-Loup Charmet/Science Photo Library **p.43** (t) Science Photo Library (b) National Library of Medicine/Science Photo Library **p.44** John Heseltine/CORBIS **p.45** (t) Dr P. Marazzi/Science Photo Library (b) John Moss/Science Photo Library